Ocean watch

Blue **Peter**

Written by
MARTYN BRAMWELL
Consultant
DR PHILIP WHITFIELD

ĐK

A Dorling Kindersley Book

Dorling DK Kindersley

LONDON, NEW YORK, SYDNEY, DELHI,
PARIS, MUNICH, and JOHANNESBURG

Project Editor Marek Walisiewicz
Art Editors Janet Allis, Amanda Carroll
Senior Editor Fran Jones
Managing Editor Sue Grabham
Senior Managing Art Editor Julia Harris
Picture Researcher Michele Faram
Production Kate Oliver and Chris Avgherinos
DTP Designer Andrew O'Brien

First published in Great Britain in 2001 by
Dorling Kindersley Limited
9 Henrietta Street
Covent Garden, London WC2E 8PS

2 4 6 8 10 9 7 5 3 1

The CIP Catalogue record for this book is available
from the British Library

ISBN 0-7513-6231-X

Reproduced by Colourscan, Singapore
Printed and bound by L.E.G.O., Italy

See our complete catalogue at
www.dk.com

Contents

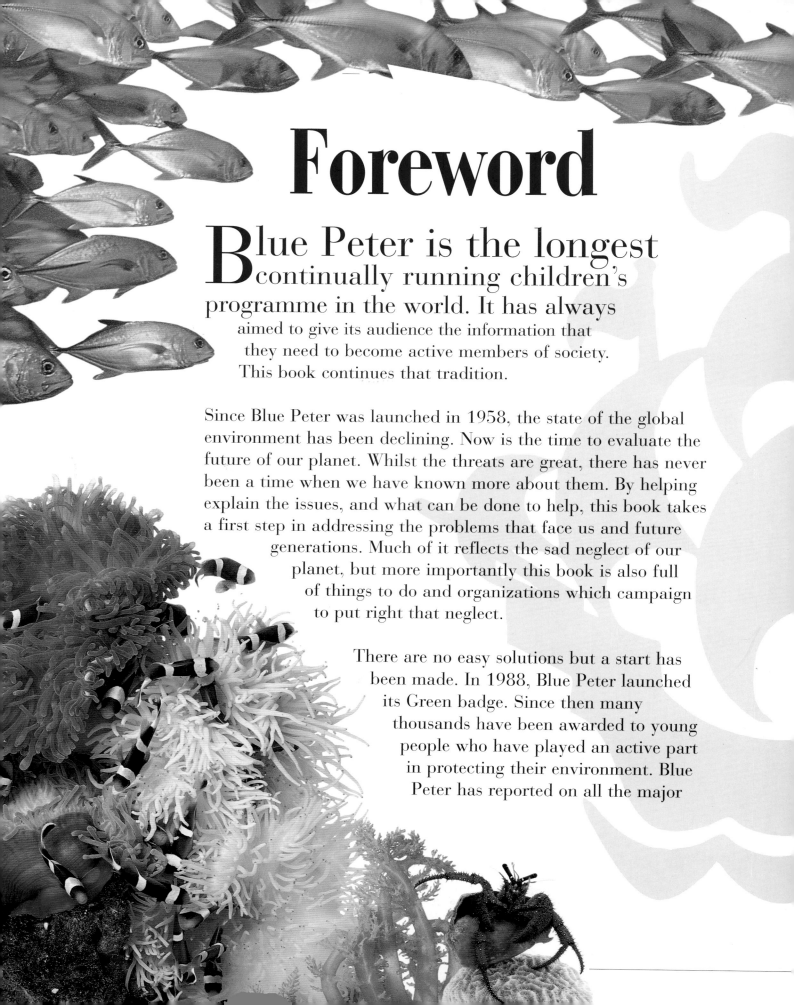

Foreword

Blue Peter is the longest continually running children's programme in the world. It has always aimed to give its audience the information that they need to become active members of society. This book continues that tradition.

Since Blue Peter was launched in 1958, the state of the global environment has been declining. Now is the time to evaluate the future of our planet. Whilst the threats are great, there has never been a time when we have known more about them. By helping explain the issues, and what can be done to help, this book takes a first step in addressing the problems that face us and future generations. Much of it reflects the sad neglect of our planet, but more importantly this book is also full of things to do and organizations which campaign to put right that neglect.

There are no easy solutions but a start has been made. In 1988, Blue Peter launched its Green badge. Since then many thousands have been awarded to young people who have played an active part in protecting their environment. Blue Peter has reported on all the major environmental initiatives of the latter part of the 20th century and has worked with many of the organizations that you will find listed at the back of this book. Blue Peter viewers have cleaned beaches, measured coastal erosion and the programme has helped to preserve its own area of coral reef. There have been enormous environmental successes in the UK, where otters and red kites have been successfully reintroduced and where recycling of household waste is now considered a part of everyday life. Now there is more to be done and today's young people will do it. You are the keepers of the Earth. You will inherit it and pass it on to generations who will be unknown to adults alive today.

"The problems may be great but, with your help, something can be done "

You have the power to change the attitudes of the adults around you. Reading this book will give you information, ideas, and people to contact who can help. The problems may be great but, with your help, something can be done.

Steve Hocking
Blue **Peter**, BBC

ONE OCEAN

THE PACIFIC, ATLANTIC, INDIAN, ARCTIC, AND SOUTHERN OCEANS ARE ALL LINKED IN ONE VAST MASS OF WATER. Together they have a huge effect on our lives. They control the weather and prevent our planet from overheating. The oceans supply most of the oxygen that we breathe, and give us great riches of food and minerals. We should start to look after them, for the sake of the future.

Hawaiian flagtails (main
picture) and Atlantic herring
(inset) are both important
links in their local food
chains. They also provide
valuable food resources for
people. But there is a big
difference. The flagtail
population is still healthy,
while in some areas the
herring have almost been
wiped out by overfishing.

" If the sea is sick, we feel it. If it dies,
we die. Our future and the future of the
oceans are one. "

DR SYLVIA EARLE
MARINE BIOLOGIST

Worlds in *motion*

The oceans are never still. Every day, the tides rise and fall, and all year round great rivers of water, called currents, swirl around the oceans. The tides are caused by the pull of the Moon as it passes overhead, but the currents are pushed along by the winds, which get their energy from the heat of the Sun. Scientists are worried that global warming (the heating of the Earth's surface) could alter winds and currents, melt the polar icecaps, and upset Earth's weather systems and climate zones.

Power of the sea

Out at sea, waves usually just rise and fall like giant ripples. They only form "white caps" when driven by strong winds. But when a wave surges up a beach, the water piles up until it topples over. Curling "breakers" are a surfer's dream, but storm waves can seriously damage harbours, sea walls, and seaside homes and farmland.

Arctic Ocean
The smallest of the oceans is covered with thick ice.

Pacific Ocean
The world's largest ocean, its deepest point is more than 11 km (6.8 miles) below the surface.

Equator

Turning up the heat

Scientists use heat-sensitive cameras in satellites to map the temperature of the oceans. The oceans absorb huge amounts of heat from the Sun. Water temperature is highest near the Equator (shown orange/red) where this heating effect is strongest. Currents then carry the warm water to colder areas (green/blue). Temperature determines what creatures live in the water.

In the **Pacific,** a **sea level** rise of just 1 m could **swamp** hundreds of low-lying **islands**

The tides

As the Moon sweeps round the Earth, the force of its gravity pulls a bulge of water towards it. (Gravity is an invisible force that "tries" to pull two objects towards one another.) The motion of the Earth also creates another bulge at the far side. These bulges cause the tides. Plants and animals that live on seashores depend on the daily rise and fall of the tide.

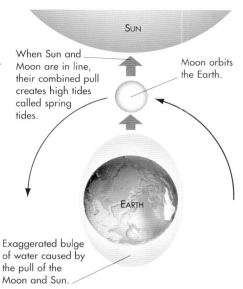

SUN

When Sun and Moon are in line, their combined pull creates high tides called spring tides.

Moon orbits the Earth.

EARTH

Exaggerated bulge of water caused by the pull of the Moon and Sun.

A seafaring nut

Coconuts are great travellers. They can stand long periods in salt water and can drift up to 4,500 km (2,800 miles) on tropical ocean currents – and still take root when they arrive on a distant beach. The plant probably originated in Polynesia in the Pacific Ocean, but has now spread throughout the tropics, riding the great ocean currents.

Ocean warming could alter **climates** on land and affect crop-growing seasons

This sea arch in England will eventually collapse from the pounding action of the waves.

Wear and tear

Pounding waves break pieces of rock from cliffs and grind them down to pebbles and eventually into fine sand. This arch formed when two wave-worn caves, on opposite sides of the headland, met in the middle. In time, the arch will collapse, leaving a pillar of rock.

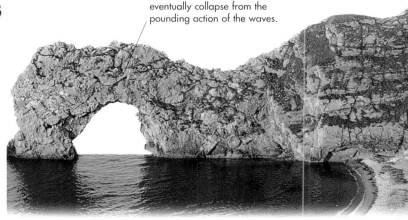

Atlantic Ocean
The saltiest of the world's oceans, it also has the highest variation between high and low tides.

Indian Ocean
Rising sea temperatures would threaten coral reefs in the waters near the Equator.

Anchovy

Plankton

Upsetting the balance

Peru's cool coastal waters are rich with plankton (tiny plants and animals) that provide food for fish. Every few years, a current of warm water, called El Niño, kills the plankton and the fish move away. The effect is disastrous because fur seals and seabirds need the fish for their survival.

Fur seal

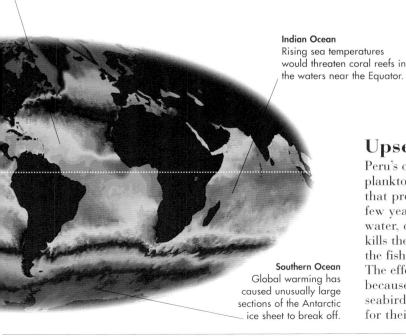

Southern Ocean
Global warming has caused unusually large sections of the Antarctic ice sheet to break off.

Birth of a storm

A hurricane starts when warm, damp air rises over a very warm patch of ocean. As the rising column of air gets bigger, it sucks in more warm air at its base, and starts to rotate. In a fully grown hurricane, the circular walls of cloud can be 20 km (12 miles) high, surrounding a calm "eye" 10–50 km (6–30 miles) across.

Storm brewing
Cloud bands begin to form around an area of low pressure.

Hurricane forming
The cloud walls thicken and the "eye" starts to show.

Mature hurricane
The full-grown hurricane moves across the China Sea.

Hurricane Alert

The most violent and destructive storms on Earth begin at sea. Known as hurricanes or cyclones, these revolving storms can be 1,000 km (620 miles) across. They form over warm, tropical seas and get their energy from the heat released when water vapour rises from the ocean and condenses into droplets. When a hurricane runs ashore it starts to weaken and die – but not before its huge store of energy is used up. Winds up to 300 kmh (190 mph), torrential rain, and huge storm waves can severely damage coastal habitats such as coral reefs and mangrove forests.

Transatlantic hitchhikers

Hurricanes can blow migratory birds and flying insects thousands of kilometres off their usual routes. American birds, such as these yellow-bellied sap-suckers, have been seen as far away as Great Britain.

Big hurricanes contain **more energy** than some countries use in a **year**

Storm surge

Giant storm waves driven by hurricane David crash against the shores of the Caribbean island of Martinique in August 1979. Homes and farmland were devastated. Millions of trees uprooted by winds and storm waves add to existing problems of soil erosion in some of the world's poorest areas.

Radar

Sensors in the nose of the plane

Strengthened wings cope with turbulence

> I live between Miami and Fort Lauderdale in Florida, an area which is known for hurricanes. Over the years, however, I've only had to deal with two hurricanes, named "Andrew" and "Floyd". While my dad was boarding up the windows to protect us from Andrew, he heard that a storm surge of 4 m (13 ft) was expected to hit between Miami and Fort Lauderdale. He said, "Our house is only 3 m (9.8 ft) above sea level. Anybody want to go to Orlando?" Mum and I were packed in about two minutes. The road was like a vast parking lot, packed with cars. In the end, the hurricane hit south Miami instead and caused terrible damage to the trees and wildlife in the area.
>
> *Danielle Bradley*

Hurricane hunter

This aircraft has been modified to investigate hurricanes. It carries extra radar above the cockpit and atmospheric sensors in the nose. The crew get a rough ride as they fly through a storm taking measurements.

Hurricane **Mitch** wiped out **70 per cent** of agriculture in **Honduras**

The aftermath

Relief workers in Honduras start to tackle the devastation left by hurricane Mitch, which tore across the Caribbean Sea in October 1998. By the time the storm passed more than 11,000 people were dead, 2.7 million were left homeless, and more than £8 billion of damage had been caused. Mitch was the deadliest hurricane to strike Central America for 200 years.

Shock waves

This destruction on the Alaska coast was caused by a giant wave in 1968. The wave was a tsunami – an enormous surge caused by an earthquake beneath the seabed of the north Pacific. Tsunamis are often called tidal waves, but they have nothing to do with tides.

Trees destroyed by the force of the tsunami.

Water spout

Tornadoes are violently spinning wind systems – a bit like hurricanes, but much narrower. On land, they can wreck houses and throw trucks into the air. At sea they suck up huge amounts of water, creating a dark-grey "pipe" like this.

Perfect BALANCE

Phytoplankton
These tiny plants drift near the sea surface. They use the Sun's energy to convert water and carbon dioxide into food.

Zooplankton
The smallest animals in the food chain include the microscopic larvae of crabs, shrimps, and other creatures.

Plants and animals that live in the sea look very different from those on land. But their ways of life and habitats are similar. Plants within the oceans do the same job as the grasslands and forests on land – they capture the Sun's energy and turn it into food. As on land, these plants provide food for grazing animals, while the grazers, in turn, provide food for the hunters. Marine habitats range from rocky and sandy shores through coral reefs and seaweed forests to the cold, dark depths of ocean basins. Communities of plants and animals have evolved to meet the challenges of each habitat. Disturbing this balance can have far-reaching effects for both animal and human life.

Ocean pastures
This satellite picture has been coloured to show the distribution of phytoplankton in the oceans. Red areas have the most, blue the least. These plants provide food for marine animals, and release oxygen into the atmosphere.

Airborne predator
Many seabirds, such as this brown pelican, feed almost entirely on small fish.

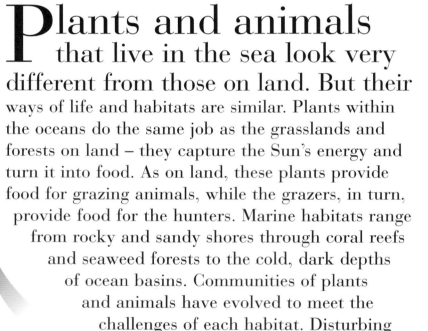

First predators
Schools of small fish, such as these anchovies, are the first of a series of predators (animals that prey on other animals).

Food chain
Every living thing needs food to fuel the processes of life – growth, development, and reproduction. A food chain is a line of feeding links between one type of creature and another. In the sunlit zones, phytoplankton grow and multiply. These tiny plants are eaten by animal plankton. Fish, such as anchovies, eat these but are eaten, in turn, by still larger fish. This continues until there is a top predator, such as a shark. A food chain need not be long. Some whales feed directly on plankton.

A drop of sea water can contain **millions** of **phytoplankton**

Fish hunters
Larger fish, such as cod, feed on the smaller fish as well as on clams, shrimps, and worms.

Squid fishing off the US coast leaves seals and dolphins short of food

Upsetting the balance

Human activities can have a disastrous effect when they upset the balance of hunters and hunted in the oceans. Fishing for sharks is a popular sport off Tasmania. Sharks feed on octopuses, and removing the sharks causes the number of octopuses to rise. Octopuses then eat more of their natural prey – spiny lobsters – and the balance is changed.

Octopus
The octopus has a powerful beak which makes short work of lobsters, snails, and shellfish.

ADAPTING TO HABITAT

EXPERIMENT

You will need: rubber gloves, 2 types of seaweed, 2 polythene bags, coloured tape, kitchen scales, pegs and line.

Colour code the seaweeds.

Store in a polythene bag.

1 WHEN YOU VISIT A ROCKY BEACH collect two small bunches of seaweed. One of the seaweeds should grow at the water's edge at low tide. The other should be gathered from near the high tide mark.

Weigh out an equal amount of each seaweed.

2 CAREFULLY WEIGH each bunch of seaweed. Remove pieces from the heavier bunch until it weighs exactly the same as the lighter bunch of seaweed.

3 HANG THE bunches out in a dry place. Weigh them daily for four days. The seaweed that grew near the water will lose weight faster than the one that grew higher up the beach.

This shows that: seaweeds that grow higher up the beach – and are out of the sea for most of the day – are better adapted for holding on to vital water.

Large sharks have only one natural enemy – humans

Top predator
This great white shark is at the top of the food chain. It can only be killed by humans, old age, or disease.

MARINE BIOLOGIST
CARL MEYER

CARL MEYER IS BASED AT THE HAWAII INSTITUTE OF MARINE BIOLOGY WHERE HE STUDIES THE SHARKS THAT THRIVE AROUND HAWAII. TRACKING THE movement of these endangered creatures takes Carl from the waters of Waikiki Marine Reserve to the turbulent Pacific Ocean.

A day in the life of a
MARINE BIOLOGIST

It is necessary to understand how far sharks roam in order to design effective conservation measures.

Mask

Scuba
Part of Carl and his colleagues' essential equipment includes underwater breathing apparatus.

Air supply tube

Compass

Depth gauge

Pressure gauge

Air tank (yellow) and reserve tank (blue)

Mouthpiece

Emergency mouthpiece

Today, Carl and his colleagues from the Shark Research Group plan to capture a large tiger shark and equip it with a sonic transmitter so that its movements can be followed.

4:00pm I collect 30 large tuna heads (bait for the evening's shark fishing trip) from a local fish market and drive to Honolulu harbour where I meet up with colleagues Aaron and Steve. We load the bait, shark fishing gear, diving and computer equipment onto our research vessel.

5:00pm First we have to double-check the boat engine and electrical systems, and radio for permission to depart. Then we leave the harbour and make the 2-km (1.24-mile) trip out to our shark fishing grounds.

5:30pm On reaching our destination we bait and place three shark longlines in 20–100 m (66–328 ft) of water. Each longline consists of ten large steel hooks, attached to a main rope line by biteproof stainless-steel cable. Longlines are anchored on the seabed and their positions are marked with surface floats. When the last line has been set we return to harbour hoping that the bloody fish heads will attract sharks during the night.

❝Calmness, patience, and intense concentration are required when working with large tiger sharks.❞

Feeding in the data
Computers are just as important as Scuba equipment for the modern marine biologist.

6:30am We leave at dawn the next morning, full of anticipation, to retrieve the longlines. Powerful jerks on the first line indicate that something large has taken a bait during the night. As we stare into the dark-blue water, a huge, green-brown shape with massive, blunt head and gigantic girth, looms suddenly out of the depths. It has the unmistakable profile of a 5 m (16.4 ft) tiger shark – luck is on our side!

A sharp dive knife is carried in a sheath.

Shark inspection
A juvenile tiger shark is closely inspected prior to release. The tiger stripes – from which this animal gets its name – are clearly visible on the flanks of this young shark.

8:00am We attempt to secure the shark alongside our 6 m (20 ft) Boston Whaler by using the hook cable and a noose around the shark's tail. As we manoeuvre the tail rope into position, the powerful shark struggles violently and it takes several attempts to slide the noose over the thrashing tail. We fight hard to roll the shark upside down and place it in a trance-like state known as "tonic immobility". After measuring the now docile shark, I use a sharp knife to pierce a small hole in the tough skin alongside the shark's

Back in the sea
Tiger sharks are carefully measured and tagged with a numbered identification tag before they are released.

dorsal fin and insert an identification tag beneath the skin. The numbered tag will allow this shark to be recognized if it is ever captured again.

8:30am Next I have to implant a 20-cm (8-in) long transmitter into the shark's gut cavity. I use a large scalpel to make a 15-cm (6-in) incision through the thick skin and muscle of the shark's belly wall. I insert the transmitter, stitch the incision closed, and remove the hook and tail rope. We turn the shark over and release it, watching it swim effortlessly away. The transmitter will gather data about the shark's movements through the ocean and send the information to special receivers anchored on the seabed.

9:30am We put on our Scuba gear, retrieve a receiver from the seabed, and download the stored data to a laptop computer.

Special equipment
The transmitter (far left) is implanted in the shark's gut cavity. The other transmitter may be fitted externally to a shark's skin.

10:30am We return to harbour, wash and stow away the equipment, and head to the lab to analyse our data. The information we have collected on tiger sharks has already been used to dissuade the Hawaii State Government from indiscriminately killing hundreds of sharks in response to shark attacks on people.

Up from the seabed
A bottom monitor, retrieved from the seabed, is washed down with fresh water before data from transmitter-equipped sharks is downloaded to a laptop.

PACIFIC OCEAN
HAWAII
OAHU
• Honolulu
MOLOKAI
• Track started
○ Track ended

Tiger shark routes
This map shows the tracks (coloured lines) of transmitter-carrying sharks off the south coast of Oahu.

Bowhead whale
8,000 remaining

Hector's dolphin
3,000–6,000 remaining

Blue whale
5,800 remaining

Finless porpoise
Numbers unknown

Whale watch

Factory ship
A minke whale is hauled up the ramp of a Japanese factory ship in the Southern Ocean. In 1994 the International Whaling Commission declared this ocean a whale sanctuary, but Japanese whalers still hunt whales there in the name of scientific research.

Voices of protest
Many people believe that whaling should be banned completely. Others think that endangered species should be protected but that other more numerous species, such as minke whales, could be hunted if the numbers caught were limited.

With their fast boats and exploding harpoons, whalers almost wiped out some of the great whales between 1850 and 1950. Although most whaling has now stopped, whales and their smaller cousins, the dolphins and porpoises, are still at risk. Chemical pollution affects species that live in enclosed seas, such as the Baltic and Mediterranean, as well as the whales that migrate along coastlines. Military exercises using depth charges also scare whales away from traditional feeding and breeding areas. But there is hope for these giants of the sea. In the early 1900s, there were only a few California grey whales. Since the species was protected in 1946, however, the population has increased to a healthy 8,000 whales.

> "Threats such as climate change and ozone depletion are becoming just as deadly as the harpoon"
>
> THE ENVIRONMENTAL INVESTIGATION AGENCY

Fin whale
46,000 remaining

Vaquita
Less than 500 remaining

Endangered whales and dolphins
Of the world's 79 species of whales, dolphins, and porpoises, two are now so endangered that they could disappear forever in the next ten years. Fifteen more could become extinct within a human lifetime.

Deep-sea fishing
fleets **rob** some species of whale of their natural **food supplies**

Blue **Peter**
ACTION!
Find out more about organizations that are fighting to end whaling and those that support it.

Always look for the "dolphin safe" label on tins of fish.

Some **airlines** refuse to carry **dolphins** destined for marine parks and **aquariums**

Safari at sea
The sight of a whale's tail fins rising out of the water is a treat for whale watchers. Tourists can take boat safaris to see whales from places like San Diego on the California coast. This kind of ecotourism does little harm as long as the boats go out in small groups and do not chase the whales. In fact, whales often swim closer for a good look at their visitors!

Sports boats
kill and injure **hundreds of** small whales **each year**

CHUKCHI SEA

ASIA

NORTH AMERICA

BERING SEA

Most whales give birth to single calves.

Arctic feeding grounds – April to November

Breeding grounds – December to April

PACIFIC OCEAN

The calf is born at the breeding grounds a year after mating takes place.

MEXICO

Baja Peninsula

Migration routes
Every year, grey whales make a 16,000-km (10,000-mile) round trip. They swim between their feeding grounds in the cold northern seas and the warm Gulf of California where they give birth to their young. A few also swim between Russia and South Korea.

Is it right?
Dolphins are very intelligent and seem to enjoy performing. However, dolphinarium pools are tiny compared with the open sea, and captive whales are never as healthy as wild ones. Some countries are phasing out these shows and returning captive whales to their natural habitats.

No fish in the *sea*

In some areas, fish such as cod and haddock have almost disappeared, and some of the world's richest fishing grounds are in trouble. The main cause of the problem is overfishing. Just 50 years ago, the total world fish catch was about 14 million tonnes a year. By 1989, this had soared to 73 million, and things have gone wrong since then. Technology – echosounders that pinpoint shoals of fish and nets big enough to swallow jumbo jets – enables today's factory trawlers to catch, process, and freeze hundreds of tonnes of fish a day.

Fishing in Sri Lanka

Traditional fisheries that use baited lines (as shown here), nets, or small boats account for almost half the fish eaten today. There is no waste – all the fish are used as food. By contrast, most of the fish caught by factory trawlers are used to make animal feed.

Great American Fish Count

Divers around the American coasts are helping conservationists. They collect information on the types of fish they see, and how many fish there are. First, volunteers are taught to identify local species. During each dive they keep records using special underwater writing slates. Later, they send in the details to the project headquarters.

"The world catch is in decline and is expected to continue to decline... "

DR MERYL WILLIAMS
DIRECTOR, INTERNATIONAL CENTRE
FOR LIVING AQUATIC RESOURCES

Harvesting the sea

Trawl nets are funnel-shaped, with a wide opening and a narrow tail, or "cod end". The cod end is where the fish collect as the net is towed through the water. An average-size net like this will hold about a tonne of fish. The huge nets used by supertrawlers can scoop up to 100 tonnes at a time.

The highly valued **bluefin tuna** has been **fished** almost to **extinction**

Icelandic herring
Strict controls have saved the herring from being wiped out in some areas.

Caribbean
Overfishing threatens red snapper, tuna, and many shark species.

Major fishing regions of the world

On the map shown right each fish represents one million tonnes of fish caught in one year. The richest fishing grounds are on continental shelves, where the water is less than 200 m (650 ft) deep. They are also found in coastal areas where cold water, rich in food, wells up from the depths. This is where herring, anchovies, cod, haddock, mackerel, and bass are found.

EUROPE

ASIA

AFRICA

NORTH AMERICA

AUSTRALIA

SOUTH AMERICA

Pacific northwest
Russia, Korea, China, Japan, and America all fish the northwest Pacific with big factory trawlers.

Peruvian fishery
In 25 years, anchoveta hauls fell from 13 million tonnes a year to just over 5 million.

Some **trawlers** throw back 40 per cent of their **catch** – **dead** and wasted

The electronic tag stores information. It is collected when the fish is caught.

Plaice tagging

This tag records information about a fish's movements between its summer feeding grounds and its winter spawning (egg-laying) grounds. Understanding fish behaviour is important to help avoid overfishing.

Dolphins in danger

Every year, thousands of dolphins drown after they become trapped in drift nets. These long nets are suspended from floats, and hang down in the water like invisible curtains. This striped dolphin is part of the unwanted haul that fishermen call "by-catch". Good management of fisheries is helping to reduce by-catch in many parts of the world.

KEITH SAUNDERS IS BASED IN BROOME, WESTERN AUSTRALIA. HIS JOB IS TO PATROL THE SEAS LOOKING FOR BOATS THAT MIGHT BE FISHING ILLEGALLY. The area of ocean he covers is vast – stretching from the Timor Sea in the north to Australia's islands in Antarctica in the south. He is also an official Marine Park Ranger.

FISHERIES OFFICER
KEITH SAUNDERS

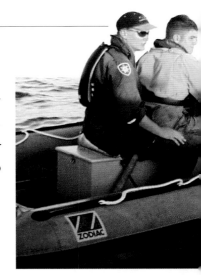

A day in the life of a
FISHERIES PROTECTION OFFICER
Fishing must be regulated to preserve fish stocks and to conserve the numbers of endangered species

Identification badge
Whenever I board a foreign fishing vessel, I introduce myself to the captain and show my identification badge.

Today, I am on duty at my office in Broome. My work is unpredictable and I can be called out to sea day or night. Our boat – the Royal Australian Navy *HMAS Geraldton* – is alongside the jetty ready to put to sea at any time.

5:00pm I receive a radio signal telling me that two foreign fishing boats have been spotted in Australian

Tuna
One of the largest fish to be caught commercially.

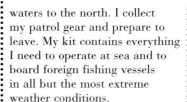

waters to the north. I collect my patrol gear and prepare to leave. My kit contains everything I need to operate at sea and to board foreign fishing vessels in all but the most extreme weather conditions.

7:00pm We set sail on the *HMAS Geraldton* and are guided to the fishing boats by coded radio signals from surveillance aircraft. We plot our route – the journey will take us a full 12 hours. This gives me plenty of time to brief the navy crew about what we will do and how to board the fishing vessels safely.

HMAS Geraldton
Our patrol boat is capable of cruising at speeds of more than 25 knots.

7:00am We reach the two boats. I board the first vessel from a Rigid Hull Inflatable Boat (RHIB) carried on board the *Geraldton* and speak to the fishermen in Indonesian. They tell me that they have not been fishing in Australian waters but are on their way to Browse Island which lies 45 km (30 miles) to the southeast. Indonesian boats are allowed to fish in an area that includes Browse Island through an agreement between the Australian and Indonesian governments called the Memorandum of Understanding (MOU).

Boarding party
The Rigid Hull Inflatable Boat is lowered from the stern deck of *HMAS Geraldton* to carry a boarding party.

After explaining the rules of fishing within the MOU area, I give the fisherman the course to the island and wish him *selemat tinggal* (goodbye). He bids me *selemat jalan* (goodbye too). We set sail for Browse Island ourselves. The island is an important nesting area for green turtles, which are protected by international law. The turtles' eggs are a popular food in Asia, and we need to check that they are not being collected illegally.

9:30am We arrive at Browse Island and go ashore to check the beaches for turtle activity. It has been a busy night and at least 50 turtles have come ashore to lay their eggs in the sand. Two of the nests have been dug up and their eggs removed – they are surrounded by human footprints that lead down to the sea. We check the fishing boats in the area but find no sign of the eggs, so we head north for Ashmore reef.

4:00pm Arrive at Ashmore, where I spend the afternoon patrolling the outer shallow reefs. As a Marine Park Ranger, I help manage the National Park which is home to many threatened species and fragile ecosystems. Animals, such as the trochus and sea cucumber that live in the sands and reefs of Ashmore, are targets for illegal fishers. Tonnes of the animals may be taken at a time, regardless of their size. Because trochus and sea cucumbers take years to grow, it is easy to wipe out whole populations very quickly by overfishing. Although we can reduce the damage by chasing and prosecuting illegal

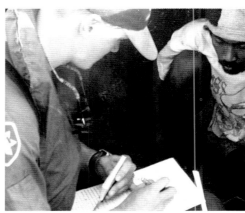

Keeping a lookout
Fisheries officers scour the vast expanses of ocean in aircraft like this Customs Coastwatch turboprop as well as in high-speed patrol boats.

Vessel inspection
On board a fishing vessel, we check that fish are not being taken illegally. We measure the size of the fish and ensure that bag limits (how many fish can be taken in one day) are not being ignored.

fishers, we know that they will return. It is our job to teach them that their activities are harmful because they will eventually wipe out the very species that they come to catch.

8:00pm We receive an urgent signal from Canberra. A Coastwatch patrol aircraft has detected an illegal vessel 160 km (100 miles) to the southeast of us outside the MOU area. We head off at full speed, setting a course to intercept them five hours later.

1:30am We board the boat and unfortunately find several tonnes of trochus shell on board. The captain agrees he has broken the law and his vessel, with its crew of 23, is towed back to Broome.

Back at Broome I will investigate the case and, if required, I will prosecute the captain and crew under the Australian Fisheries Management Act. If found guilty the captain can lose the boat and will have to pay a large fine. However, we are working with the local fishers and trying to help them understand the need to protect the different species that live in the world's oceans.

Trochus
The trochus is sought after for jewellery, buttons, and ornaments.

❝Only with the help of fishers can we protect the biological diversity of the sea.❞

Fishing area
Within the MOU zone, only traditional fishing – without help from mechanical equipment – is allowed.

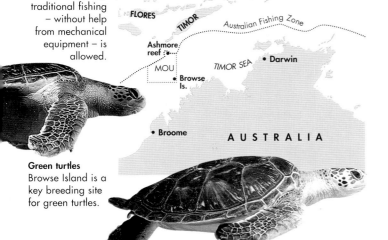

JAVA SEA
INDONESIA
FLORES
TIMOR
Australian Fishing Zone
Ashmore reef
MOU
TIMOR SEA
• Darwin
• Browse Is.
• Broome
AUSTRALIA

Green turtles
Browse Island is a key breeding site for green turtles.

Trochus buttons

Sea cucumber
The sea cucumber, or trepang, is eaten as a delicacy in Asia.

EXPLOITING *the* SEA

The oceans have always provided people with food. Today, there are other important industries that rely on raw materials from the sea. Oil and gas are extracted from rocks beneath the ocean floor, and tin and titanium are dredged from coastal sand bars. Certain seaweeds are gathered and used in processed foods, while sea water itself is treated to make clean drinking water as well as salt. The deep ocean floors are littered with fist-sized nodules rich in manganese, copper, and nickel. They are not exploited yet – but they could prove important mineral resources of the future.

Fish farming

In many countries, fish are reared in wire-mesh pens. Although fish farming reduces the numbers of fish caught in the wild, it does have problems. Here, fish food has caused a blanket of algae to grow near the pens. This algae can choke natural life nearby.

Energy from the sea

Almost a quarter of the oil and gas we use comes from beneath the shallow seas of the continental shelves. The oil and gas are extracted by drilling down through the rocks from huge platforms, such as this one in the North Sea. Oil platform workers check constantly for leaks and spills that could harm the environment.

Seaweed farming

Cultivating seaweed is a major industry in parts of Asia. In Japan, people eat more seaweed than anywhere else in the world. It is cultivated in shallow, coastal seas. In the Philippines, seaweeds are used to make carrageenan. This is a thickening and binding agent used in sausages, yoghurt, shampoos, cosmetics, and toothpastes.

Drugs that could help fight **cancer** have been extracted from **sponges**

Salt from the sea

A worker in Thailand rakes sea salt into piles. Extracting the salt is a slow business. Sea water is channelled through a series of shallow ponds where sunshine and wind evaporate the water. This makes the brine (salty water) more and more concentrated. After 18 months, the bed of the final pond is covered in a layer of glistening white salt crystals.

Fish farms around the world **provide** us with more than **4 million** tonnes of fish a year

For safety, waste gas is burned off at the end of a long boom.

Fresh water

Around the world, about 13,000 desalination (de-salting) plants produce fresh water from salt water. Desalination plants are expensive, but in desert areas they are often the only solution to water shortages. This installation in Dubai is one of 35 big plants in the United Arab Emirates.

HOW SALTY IS THE SEA?

You will need: greaseproof paper, baking tray, plastic bottle, sea water, magnifying glass.

Sea water collected during a trip to the coast.

1 LINE THE BAKING TRAY with greaseproof paper. Press the paper well down into the corners and turn it up at the edges so that it can hold water.

2 POUR IN ABOUT half a litre (1 pint) of sea water. Leave the tray in a warm place, such as an airing cupboard or on a sunny window ledge.

3 WHEN ALL THE WATER has evaporated, examine the dried salt crystals under a magnifying glass. Most of the crystals will be cube-shaped.

This shows that: the sea is full of salt minerals. Most of this is the same chemical as table salt.

EXPERIMENT

CORAL REEFS

AND COASTLINES

66 Corals do not appear to be able to adapt fast enough to keep pace with changes in ocean temperature. 99

PROFESSOR OVE HOEGH-GULDBERG
UNIVERSITY OF SYDNEY, AUSTRALIA

CORAL REEFS, BEACHES, SALT MARSHES, AND MANGROVE SWAMPS ARE COMPLEX PLACES DELICATELY balanced between the sea and the land. They are vital to the planet's well-being, but also very fragile – vulnerable to storm damage, overfishing, pollution, and tourists, as well as environmental changes.

Kayangel (main picture) is a typical atoll in the western Pacific. A ring of coral reefs, just below sea level, encloses a lagoon, while sand has piled up on parts of the reef to create small islands. Even a 1 m (3.3 ft) rise in sea level would cover hundreds of atolls like this. The inset picture shows a Red Sea coral reef damaged by tourists taking souvenirs.

Reef in DANGER

Two-thirds of reefs in the Caribbean are threatened by over-harvesting and pollution

Coral reefs are the richest habitats in the ocean. Just a few kilometres of reef can contain well over 3,000 species – from minute shrimps to fish weighing more than half a tonne. A reef is a massive, rocky structure but it is also surprisingly fragile. The tiny animals, called polyps, which build the reef can only thrive when conditions are just right. The water must be shallow enough for sunlight to reach the coral, and the water should be at least 18°C (65°F) warm. It must also be free from mud and pollution. Any change in these conditions puts the reef at risk.

The living reef

A coral reef swarms with life. With all its nooks and crannies it provides a home for hundreds of different types of marine plants and animals as well as the living corals themselves. The reef is a complete ecosystem in its own right – a complex world where scavengers, filter-feeders, plant-eaters, and hunters all depend on one another for survival.

Tentacles are armed with stinging cells.

There is just one body opening.

Each polyp makes its own skeleton cup.

Only the surface of the reef is alive.

The reef builds up layer by layer.

Reef builders

A reef is built from the piled-up skeletons of tiny animals called polyps. Each polyp makes a hard limestone cup to live in – poking out its tentacles to feed, and pulling back inside when danger comes along. When the polyps die, their skeletons remain. These gradually build up to create a coral reef.

Brain coral

Organ-pipe coral

Staghorn coral

Bleached coral

These scientists are studying bleached corals in Polynesia, in the Pacific Ocean. Corals get some of their colour from tiny algae that live inside them. If the water temperature rises, or the reef is polluted, the algae leave and the coral turns white. If the right conditions do not return quickly, the reef will die.

Anchor damage

Reefs suffer a great deal of damage when tourist boats lower anchors and chains to the sea floor (shown here). Although the old limestone rock at the heart of a reef is tough enough to rip the bottom out of a ship, the thin layer of living coral on the surface of the reef is delicate.

A market for coral

Corals grow in a range of appealing shapes and colours, and thousands of tonnes are sold every year to tourists. This Bali islander is collecting a basket of dead coral to sell. Each time a lump of coral is sold, another piece is hacked off a reef to take its place on the market stall. It can take decades for the coral to regrow.

> " Pollution, overfishing, and overuse have put many of our unique reefs at risk... "
>
> BILL CLINTON
> US PRESIDENT (1993–2001)

Some of the world's coral reefs may be 2.5 million years old

Mining reefs for building materials continues in the Indian Ocean

Blue Peter
ACTION!
If you are diving or snorkelling on a reef, look – but never touch.

Do not buy souvenirs made of coral, rare shells, or parts of other reef creatures.

Island REFUGE

When British naturalist Charles Darwin visited the Galápagos Islands in 1835, he discovered giant tortoises, iguanas that fed on seaweed, and cormorants that could not fly. Darwin soon realized that each species had adapted to the special set of conditions on its island home. This discovery led him to his theory of evolution. Islands are still home to unusual species, but many have been wiped out by cats and rats introduced from visiting ships. People have also destroyed habitats in their search for timber and minerals or by taking land for farming.

Island giant

At 3 m (10 ft) long and 136 kg (300 lb) in weight, the Komodo dragon is the world's largest lizard. It lives on Komodo Island in Indonesia, and eats deer, bush pigs, eggs, and carrion. Hunters almost wiped out the dragon, but the 5,000 that remain are now protected by law.

Animals brought to islands by **people** cause **70** per cent of **extinctions** of **native** species

Birth of an island

In 1963 a volcano erupted 130 m (425 ft) down on the floor of the Atlantic Ocean off the coast of Iceland. Gradually, ash and lava built up higher and higher until the tip of the volcano burst through the surface of the water. A new island – Surtsey – was born. Two years later, wind-blown seeds had taken root and the first insects and birds had arrived.

By 1990, there were 20 different plant species growing on Surtsey.

Once plants were established, birds began to nest on the island.

Blue Peter

ACTION!

Support local and international conservation organizations that help protect island habitats.

When visiting islands, respect the local wildlife.

Crazy ants
These ants get their name from their habit of dashing about in constant frantic activity.

Ant attack

In 1998, scientists discovered that crazy ants – a species accidentally introduced to Bird Island in the Seychelles – had become a serious problem. They had infested the nests of sooty terns and driven away 60,000 breeding pairs of these birds. Now, ant control measures are being planned.

Birds in...
Kaka numbers on Kapiti Island have grown since the removal of alien species.

Kaka

...Aliens out
Alien species removed from Kapiti included 22,500 possums.

Possum

Habitat destruction

Christmas Island in the Indian Ocean has been devastated by phosphate mining. To get at the deposits, miners have to cut down the dense rainforest cover, and then dig out the phosphate. This leaves a desolate landscape of bare limestone rock. The destruction has endangered several rare seabirds that nest in the tall trees, and also several land birds.

> I live in Paekakariki, New Zealand, and from my house I see Kapiti Island, the native bird reserve. To get there you need a permit and go on a special boat. There are no possums, dogs, or cats, so the birds aren't eaten. There are the blue takahe that can't fly like the spotted kiwi. You don't see this kiwi in the day, though, because it sleeps then. The kaka sit on your head and eat from your hand. The birds eat the berries from the native trees, and the insects. You are allowed to take only photos and leave only foot prints!

Rehua Watson.

Cash clearance

This banana plantation on the Caribbean island of Martinique shows a problem common to many tropical islands. Most of the original vegetation has been cleared to make room for crops that local farmers can sell to developed countries. This robs native birds, mammals, and insects of their natural habitats and food supplies.

Takahe

Kapiti nature reserve

Kapiti Island, about 5 km (3 miles) off the southwest tip of North Island, New Zealand, has been made into a bird sanctuary. It was a huge task that took several years. To make the island safe for rare native birds such as the kaka and takahe, thousands of non-native predators including possums, cats, weasels, and rats, were removed. Habitat-destroying domestic animals such as goats, sheep, and cattle were also removed.

MARINE BIOLOGIST
AMANDA VINCENT

DR AMANDA VINCENT IS CO-DIRECTOR OF PROJECT SEAHORSE, AN INTERNATIONAL GROUP OF BIOLOGISTS AND SOCIAL WORKERS WHO ARE TRYING TO SECURE a safe future for seahorses and their habitats. She works with a Filipino team on a community project based in the traditional fishing village of Handumon.

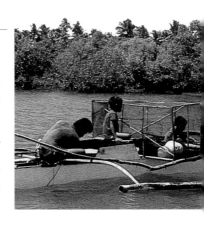

A day in the life of a
SEAHORSE SPECIALIST

Project Seahorse is committed to conserving seahorses and their habitats while respecting human needs.

Today, I'm in Handumon in the central Philippines. I plan to go looking for seahorses with the local fishers. It is a world away from my life in Montreal, Canada, where I teach at McGill University.

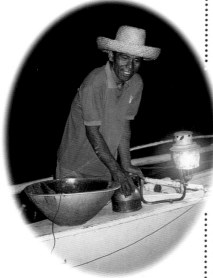

Lighting the way
A seahorse fisher lights the lantern that will help him to spot seahorses in the still-dark hours of early morning.

1:00am A seahorse fisher calls through the bamboo walls of our staff house to see if I'm awake. He then waits as I struggle into my wetsuit. We make our way out through the mangroves and into his small outrigger boat. He lights the lantern and starts paddling towards the dim outline that is Mahanay Island.

2:30am The fisher and I slide into the water. We position ourselves on either side of the bow under the lantern and swim slowly ahead, scanning the bottom for fish and crabs. He spears anything that he thinks he can sell later, twisting seahorses off their perches before popping them into a small container on the boat.

5:00am Our swimming has slowed greatly. The fisher and I are both feeling despondent. Years of overfishing means there really isn't much to catch, or many seahorses left to spot. The dawn comes up slowly and we clamber into the boat,

cold and tired. The fisher will sell the seahorses to buyers in the village. From there, live ones will be sold to aquarium collectors, while dead ones will be sold as ornaments. They are also used as ingredients for traditional Chinese medicines (seahorses are believed to cure illnesses such as asthma). The demand for seahorses is great. Worldwide, tens of millions are

caught every year, which has caused their numbers to fall in many areas. Relatively little is known about the biology of seahorses, and part of my work here is to study how their populations respond to fishing.

6:00am We arrive home at Handumon and head up to the staff house. The team biologists and village

Studying the catch
Fishers bring their catch of seahorses to the staff house every day. Here, Marivic and I are sorting and measuring them.

Taking measurements
Before you can measure a seahorse, you have to coax it to straighten its tail. The size of the seahorses is noted while the coloured tag tells us their age.

Positioning a seahorse cage
Unusually, it is male seahorses who carry their young. The males are protected in a cage until they give birth.

Fair craft
The team's community adviser, Mia, displays crafts that earn extra income for seahorse-fishing families.

trainees measure, weigh, and document the seahorses the fisher caught. These few animals will earn half his pay for that night. Another important part of our work here is to build the support of the local people. If we are to succeed in protecting the seahorses and their habitats, it's no good just telling the fishers to stop taking the animals, because seahorses are their livelihood.

6:30am More fishers arrive. We grab hot drinks and sit talking on the balcony. The topic for discussion is poaching. The village has set up a 33-hectare (82-acre) marine sanctuary where no fishing of any kind is permitted. There is an adjacent zone where only fishing with traditional methods is allowed. Both are patrolled by the villagers, but poachers still strike, attracted by the larger catches in these areas.

Seahorse seas
The tiny village of Handumon lies just to the west of Talibon on the island of Bohol in the Philippines.

8:30am Breakfast at last – rice and fish as usual. Our high school apprentices arrive. They work with us every weekend, helping with our conservation projects in exchange for scholarships that allow them to continue in school. Today our community organizer, Mia, is helping them develop a puppet show to teach young children about environmental issues. I work with them a bit, making them laugh at my mistakes in the local Cebuano language.

Male seahorse
This adult, big-bellied seahorse can inflate his pouch to attract females during courtship.

10:30am Jonathan, the lead biologist, and I go to look at the seahorses in a protected study site beyond the next island. The village assistant helps us load our outrigger boat, Project Seahorse, with dive gear, food, and water. Then he steers us out through the nearby mangrove plantation.

11:00am We plunge into the water and start looking for seahorses that we have previously fitted with tags. They are difficult to spot, but we eventually find most of them. We note the tag number on their collars, their location, their reproductive state, and their behaviour. It is slow and careful work, and we only pause to eat.

❝Our vision is a world where populations of seahorses are secure.❞

New generation
This newborn seahorse is 8 mm (0.03 in) long. Seahorses hang on to algae and corals with their tails.

5:00pm We arrive home, wash the gear, then start entering the new data in our computers. We have no permanent electricity supply at Handumon, so we hope that our solar power will last until we have finished. The team leader, Marivic, reviews the day over supper.

7:00pm We plan for a meeting with the municipal officials tomorrow. We will ask them to give more support to the villagers who are trying so hard to manage their marine resources wisely. I desperately need sleep but must complete my reports before I can rest.

COASTAL *Care*

At the boundary between land and sea, the coasts provide a huge variety of habitats for some of the most fascinating animals and plants on our planet. But coasts also attract people in vast numbers – many come on holiday, others to find permanent homes. This increases the level of development and pollution in these areas. However, worldwide beach clean-up events are helping to preserve the world's coastlines. The projects help people to understand the problems and enable them to do something positive.

Survival techniques

The coast is a harsh place. Seaside plants must cope with salt spray – and must also survive on shifting sands, or tiny amounts of soil in rock crevices. Many have short stems and cushion-like leaves to protect them from the buffeting and drying effect of the wind. To avoid the sun and marauding seabirds, worms and cockles burrow into the sand when the tide goes out, while limpets clamp themselves to the rocks and crabs hide under fronds of damp seaweed.

Cliff tops
Short grasses grow in the thin soil. Puffins and Manx shearwaters nest in cliff-top burrows.

Rockpools
Home to crabs, limpets, anemones, and starfish, the rock pools are filled with many seaweeds.

Sandy beach
Hundreds of species of worms and shellfish live hidden in their burrows beneath the sand.

Rocky headlands
Birds such as kittiwakes, guillemots, and razorbills nest on narrow cliff ledges.

Marram dunes

The shifting surface of a sand dune is a difficult place for any plant to take root. However, marram grass grows quickly and has roots that spread sideways as well as down. This helps to anchor the sand and allows other plants to get established.

Dense roots bind loose sand grains together.

"I live in New Jersey, USA, right near Atlantic City. The beach here has changed a lot over the years. When my parents were kids it was clean, but now the water pollution is so bad that fish often wash up dead. If you walk along the beach, you find broken bottles, plastic cups, and even cigarette ends. Because I care about the beach, I do voluntary work with a group called Clean Ocean Action who try to protect the ocean. This makes the beach a better place for the animals that live there – and for the people too."

Jenna Gatto

Blue Peter
ACTION!
Cut through plastic six-pack yokes before throwing them away.

Find out how you can take part in a local beach-cleaning project.

Beach clean-up

In many countries, young people take part in beach clean-up operations. The detailed surveys carried out during these events show what the main types of rubbish are and where they come from. This helps governments make better enviromental laws.

Lethal litter

Of all the litter that people leave on beaches, the most dangerous are plastic bags and yokes that hold drinks cans. Birds and even young seals get their heads or legs caught in them. This can lead to them drowning or being strangled.

This American coot is caught in the plastic loops of a six-pack yoke.

Seabird sanctuary

The eggs and nestlings of some species, like these little terns, are often well camouflaged. This means they are almost impossible to see against a background of pebbles – until it's too late. Look out for notices that ask you to keep off beaches where birds are breeding.

Chemical beach

Occasionally a metal drum, or a plastic container of liquid or powder, may wash up on a beach. It could contain acid or poisonous chemicals – and might even be giving off dangerous fumes. This is no ordinary beach rubbish and should not be approached. Tell a parent or teacher.

The human tide

Bournemouth beach, in southern England, is packed with tourists in summer – up to 100,000 of them on 11 km (7 miles) of sandy beach. Every morning and evening a team of 25 workers with hand rakes and tractor-powered machines cleans the entire beach, shifting up to 20 tonnes of flotsam and litter a day. This clean-up costs huge amounts of money.

Scarce water

Goa, on the west coast of India, is a tourist paradise with long sandy beaches fringed with palm trees. But here, and in many other tropical resorts, there's a price to pay. Big hotels with lush gardens are often allowed to take a huge share of scarce fresh water resources, leaving little for the local people.

TOURIST TRAFFIC

Within ten years more than a billion people will be taking their annual holidays abroad. Many countries – especially those with beautiful beaches and coral reefs – depend on tourists to provide a living income for their people. But tourism brings problems, too. Building airports, roads, and hotels, providing enough fresh water, and disposing of sewage all have an effect on coastal environments. Also, the sheer numbers of visitors can threaten local habitats and wildlife. Tourism is important, and here to stay, but it needs to be very carefully planned. Responsible "ecotourism" may help to reduce visitors' impact on the environment.

A big **hotel** uses as much **electricity** as 3,500 medium-sized **households**

Dangerous sports

Water skiing, power-boating, and jet-skiing are great fun, but they can also endanger wildlife. In some holiday resorts they are restricted to certain zones to keep them away from colonies of seals, otters, dolphins, and diving birds, such as cormorants and pelicans.

> # "The rapid growth of tourism around the Mediterranean Sea is a major threat to the environment and biodiversity of the area."
>
> UNITED NATIONS
> ENVIRONMENT PROGRAMME
> EARTHSCAN 2000

Sea urchin

Starfish

Sea sponge

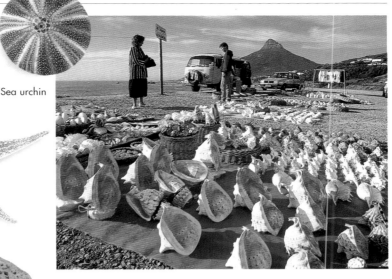

Beware what you buy

Beautiful shells are for sale on this beach in South Africa. If the trader only collects empty shells for sale, no harm is done, but in many parts of the world, unscrupulous dealers hunt living shellfish, sea turtles, and rare species of starfish, sea urchins, and sponges. If in doubt, do not buy. You could be breaking international laws.

All visitors to **Belize** are charged a small **fee** — the **money** is used to pay for **nature** conservation

Endangered species

This green sea turtle has hatched on a tropical beach, and must dash to the sea past marauding seabirds. Even then it is not safe. Hunters kill adult turtles for meat and shells. Also, when adult females come ashore to lay their eggs, there are more dangers from illegal egg collectors, and thoughtless tourists who trespass on protected beaches.

Blue Peter
ACTION!

Never be tempted to pick plants or flowers that are growing wild.

Stay on marked paths and keep your distance from wildlife.

Always take litter home with you after a day at the beach.

MARINE MAMMAL MEDIC
KIERAN COPELAND

KIERAN COPELAND WORKS AT THE SOS SEAL RESCUE HOSPITAL BASED AT HUNSTANTON IN ENGLAND. THROUGHOUT THE YEAR, THE HOSPITAL CARES FOR sick or abandoned seals, as well as porpoises and, occasionally, whales. The aim of the hospital is to rehabilitate the seals before releasing them back into the wild.

Seal colony, North Sea
Pups are released as close as possible to where they were rescued – usually near a wild colony such as this.

A day in the life of a
MARINE MAMMAL MEDIC

By understanding more about the behaviour of seals, we are better prepared to help with their long-term conservation.

Today, Kieran and his colleagues face a routine day of health checks and feeding. They never know, however, when they may get a call to go out and rescue a seal or seal pup from a nearby beach.

Hunstanton
Common and grey seals live in wild colonies along the North Sea coast.

12:00am Midnight and my shift starts. When I arrive at the Sea Life Aquarium, I feed the latest seal pup casualties in the hospital here. Seal pups are taken in for a variety of reasons. They may have been abandoned by their mothers, damaged by fishing nets, or are sick. We have three pups at the moment, and they need to be fed every four hours. Feeding is a tricky business as I have to insert a tube down one pup's throat so I can pour in a fatty milk substitute. The pup is still too young to take proper food. The other pups have learned to feed for themselves, so I toss them a fish and let them get on with it.

4:00am Same procedure as at midnight with the whole process taking about 30 minutes. The pups in the hospital have to progress through a number of stages of rehabilitation before they are ready for release. If unweaned, they start off on force-fed milk substitute and then fish until they are able to eat for themselves. Next they will be introduced to our resident seals and will learn to compete for their food. The pups need to weigh at least 35 kg (77 lb) before we can release them back in the sea. Depending on their injuries, it can take 3–6 months before the pup is fit.

Teeth check
Despite their endearing image, seal pups have strong teeth.

Eye check
Seals may arrive with ulcers in their eyes. Quick treatment prevents what could become a serious problem.

8:00am I am first to arrive and open up. I check the pups have not deteriorated before feeding them again. My assistant Barney arrives and prepares the aquarium for opening to the public at 10 am. As well as the seals, the aquarium has more than 30 displays, mainly focusing on British marine life.

There's a lot to clean and check. I prepare the treatment schedules for the day and go to treat one of the seals that has an eye infection. The seals' temperatures are also taken, and several other checks completed. Barney and I then grab some breakfast while chatting about how the pups are progressing and our plans for the rest of the day.

10:30am Time for the daily environmental enrichment activities for the resident seals. These are common seals that, for many reasons, would not survive if they were released back into the wild. Fish pulls, ice blocks, and seaweed are designed to make the animals search out and work for their fish. The seals seem to enjoy the exercise and visitors love watching them racing and splashing around.

Feeding time
Once they have learned to eat for themselves, seal pups enjoy regular meals of herring or mackerel.

12:00pm Time to feed the pups again. They've got ravenous appetites at this age and get through 3 kg (6.6 lb) of herring a day. The aquarium rescues on average 25 pups every year. They're mostly common pups but we do get the occasional grey seal in the winter.

Injured seal pup
It is important to approach the seal pup with care as it will be scared.

12:30pm A phone call comes through from a member of the public to report an injured pup washed up on a beach. I ask the caller a number of questions to ascertain the exact location of the pup. I also ask about its condition. The pup sounds in poor health so I tell the caller not to touch the pup, but to keep people away and wait until I get there. I load the pup rescue equipment into the van and head off towards Weybourne which is about an hour away.

1:30pm When I arrive, I find a one-month-old female grey seal pup with a suspected parasite infestation and a dog bite on her back. Although they have the image of being cute and docile, seal pups have quite a nasty bite and can carry viruses that are transferable to humans. I carefully load the pup into a carrying cage and put her into the van. Once back, I let the pup rest for a while after her traumatic journey.

"Our best years are the quiet ones as this means there have been fewer seals injured or abandoned."

4:30pm Time to check the pup into our hospital. First I take her temperature and then spray antiseptic onto the wounds. This temporarily turns the skin a strange, green colour. The pup is weighed with the assistance of Barney and then we monitor her breathing and heart rate. I also take blood samples and send them to the lab where they are checked for viruses or infection.

Checking the lungs
Every pup admitted to the hospital undergoes an examination for health problems.

Weighing the seal pup
Barney weighs the seal pup. We need to monitor how well the seals are putting on weight before they can be released.

5:15pm I take fish out of the freezer to defrost for tomorrow's feeds, then clean and shut down the hospital. It is important to follow strict procedures in order to keep the hospital sterile and reduce the risk of infection for both seals and humans. By 6 pm it's time to lock up. It's been a long day, but with increasing pressure on the marine environment the rescue, rehabilitation, and release work will help safeguard the future of Britain's marine mammals.

Resident seals
Seals that are unable to survive in the wild are offered a permanent home at the centre.

Wetland

Swamps and mangrove forests, salt marshes and mudflats are strange

places, halfway between land and sea. Most are muddy and some stink of rotting vegetation. But they are very, very important. Wetlands protect the coast from waves and tides, and provide sheltered spawning grounds for shellfish and fish. They have rich feeding areas for birds, especially long-distance migrants, and also offer a safe haven for many rare plants, insects, frogs, and other creatures. They can even filter out some pollutants. But like all habitats, wetlands are fragile and can be damaged.

Trees on stilts

Forests of mangroves, like this one in Indonesia, cover shorelines throughout the tropics. Their tangled, stilt-like roots trap silt, helping to build up the land. In parts of Asia, almost 70 per cent of the mangroves have been cut down to make way for fish- and shrimp-farming ponds, leaving the coast vulnerable to storms and tidal waves.

Wetlands take up about six per cent of the Earth's land surface

Saltwater crocodile

The 5 m (16 ft) American crocodile lives in estuaries and mangrove swamps in Florida. Once threatened by hunting, its numbers are now increasing. However, it still suffers from habitat destruction and illegal hunting.

The Sundarbans wetlands contain one of India's biggest tiger reserves

Watch

Choking invader

The water hyacinth – a native of tropical America – has become a serious problem worldwide. The plant grows very quickly, choking rivers, lakes, and coastal lagoons. The floating vegetation can cover the entire water surface. This robs other plants of the light they need and starves fish of oxygen.

Dense, fibrous roots absorb oxygen and nutrients from the water.

Disaster in Spain

Workers take poisoned fish from a river near the Coto Doñana National Park in Spain in 1998. The disaster occurred when 5 million cubic metres (177 million cubic feet) of mud containing toxic metals spilled from a sludge pond at a mineral mine. The spill affected rare species such as the gecko lizard, otter, and lynx.

Rare species such as this white stork – as well as the imperial eagle – were threatened.

Innocent victim

A manatee or "sea cow" shows the terrible scars caused by sports-boat propellers. This large, slow, gentle plant-eater is found in bays, estuaries, and coastal lagoons in Florida and the Caribbean. It is protected by law, but still suffers from boat injuries, poaching, and even sudden temperature changes.

Staging post

Thousands of knots (small, plump shorebirds) wheel above the mudflats of the Wash in East Anglia. The birds breed in the Arctic tundra but fly south to spend the winter on the coasts of western Europe and even as far south as West Africa. Coastal wetlands like these are vital feeding areas for many types of migrant birds.

By 1999, **116 countries** had signed an **international** agreement to **protect** the world's wetlands

" I live in a remote village on the Norfolk coast in England. The village overlooks salt marshes that attract different types of birds – some from overseas. The Norfolk Wildlife Trust have a bird reserve where people can watch rare birds from hides (small huts with peepholes). Sadly, the birds' homes are under threat from strong tides breaking through the shingle bank and flooding the marshes, the roads, and people's homes. Some people make a living by cutting down reeds that grow in the marsh. These are used to thatch roofs. "

J. W. Groom

OCEANS AT RISK

> **"** The reality is that my country's pollution needs no visa to visit your country – just a favourable current. **"**

ROBERT HILL
FEDERAL ENVIRONMENT MINISTER, AUSTRALIA

MORE POLLUTION HAS BEEN DUMPED AT SEA IN THE PAST CENTURY THAN IN THE PREVIOUS 2,000 years. The cocktail of sewage, chemicals, oil, nuclear and solid waste is poisoning our coasts and spreading far out into the oceans. Action is needed now – growing populations are set to make the problems worse.

A huge breaker thunders towards Oahu Island in Hawaii (main picture). The water looks crystal clear, but even here in the mid-Pacific, far from the world's industrial centres, the ocean contains traces of industrial chemicals that pollute coastal waters and affect fisheries. The smaller picture shows why.

Chemical Pollution

A cid fumes from factory chimneys, pesticides and fertilizers from farmland, and poisons that seep from waste dumps are all types of chemical pollution. At first they do not seem to have much to do with the oceans, which may be hundreds of kilometres away. However, the land and the sea are linked together by rivers, and by rainwater seeping through the ground. Whatever we spill, throw away, burn, or bury eventually mingles with the water and begins its journey to the sea. These chemicals affect living things in ways that we do not understand. For this reason, some governments are now passing laws to try and prevent the dumping of pollutants into the world's waters.

Chemical sprays

Farmers and foresters often spray chemical pesticides to protect their crops and trees from insect pests. The problem is that some of these chemicals can remain in the environment long after they have done their job. They may get washed into rivers where they can damage plant and animal life.

Agro-chemicals
Pesticides and fertilizers can harm the environment.

Acid rain
Chemicals in factory smoke can dissolve in rainwater to form acid rain which damages trees and soil.

Salt water
When salt is put onto roads in winter, it can wash into rivers and kill the freshwater fish.

Journey to the sea

Some pollutants break down into harmless substances before they ever reach the sea. Others – such as metals from industrial processes and pesticides – build up in the environment. Also, fertilizers, detergents, and sewage add nutrients to the water that cause rapid growth of algae, relatives of the seaweeds. This uses up all the oxygen which, in turn, kills the fish.

Blue Peter ACTION!

Never throw litter, such as cans or bottles, into rivers or seas.

Recycle whatever you can.

Report any coloured or smelly river water to the local authority.

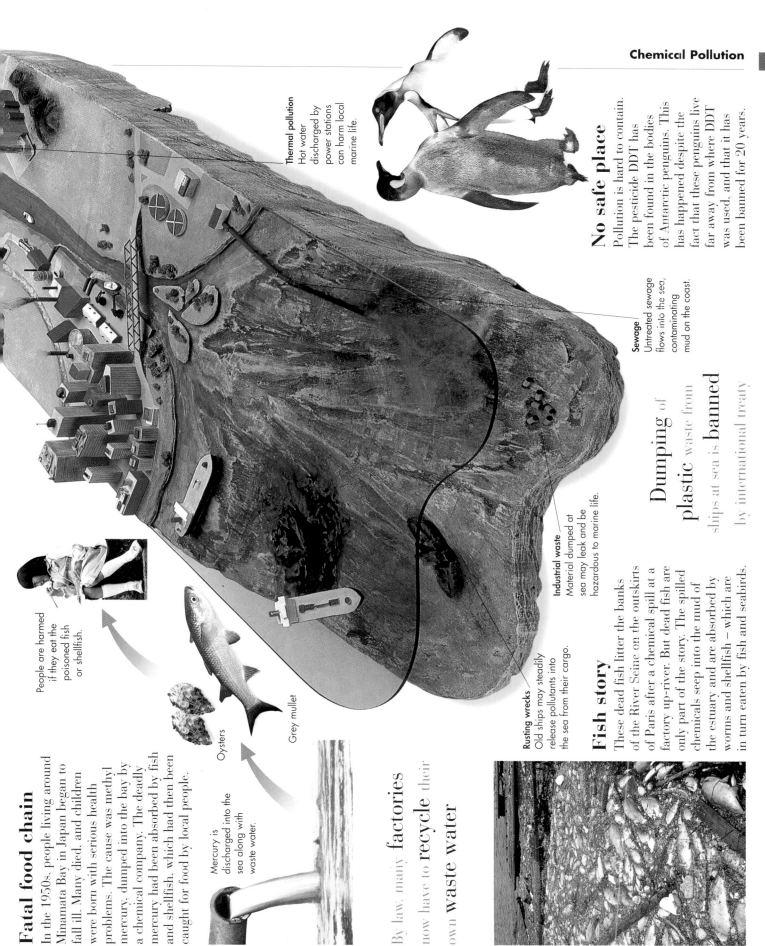

Thermal pollution
Hot water discharged by power stations can harm local marine life.

Sewage
Untreated sewage flows into the sea, contaminating mud on the coast.

Industrial waste
Material dumped at sea may leak and be hazardous to marine life.

Rusting wrecks
Old ships may steadily release pollutants into the sea from their cargo.

Mercury is discharged into the sea along with waste water.

Grey mullet

Oysters

People are harmed if they eat the poisoned fish or shellfish.

No safe place

Pollution is hard to contain. The pesticide DDT has been found in the bodies of Antarctic penguins. This has happened despite the fact that these penguins live far away from where DDT was used, and that it has been banned for 20 years.

Dumping of plastic waste from ships at sea is banned by international treaty

Fish story

These dead fish litter the banks of the River Seine on the outskirts of Paris after a chemical spill at a factory up-river. But dead fish are only part of the story. The spilled chemicals seep into the mud of the estuary and are absorbed by worms and shellfish – which are in turn eaten by fish and seabirds.

Fatal food chain

In the 1950s, people living around Minamata Bay in Japan began to fall ill. Many died, and children were born with serious health problems. The cause was methyl mercury, dumped into the bay by a chemical company. The deadly mercury had been absorbed by fish and shellfish, which had then been caught for food by local people.

By law, many factories now have to recycle their own waste water

Whatever goes down a drain ends up in the big sink – the ocean

Tainted waters

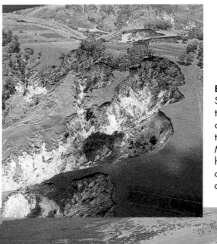

Erosion scars
Stripped of their protective covering of trees, these hills in Madagascar show how rainwater can quickly wash away the soil.

Sometimes pollution is obvious. Rivers near copper and iron mines may be stained by metals seeping from waste dumps. Rivers and shorelines can become covered by frothy scum that forms when chemicals and farm fertilizers run into the water. Too much mud in a river is also a form of pollution because it can choke delicate coastal habitats. But even more deadly is the pollution we cannot see. When dangerous chemicals are spilled or buried on land, they slowly filter into the water deep below the ground. It may take many years, but they eventually end up in rivers – and the sea. We must endeavour to protect the seas from becoming tainted with pollutants.

River of mud
After a night of heavy rain, this river in Haiti stains the sea brown with soil swept off the deforested slopes inland.

Choking reefs
Once beautiful coral reefs are suffocated under a blanket of mud washed down by the river.

Every year, **erosion** robs the **Earth** of 25 billion **tonnes** more **topsoil** than it produces

Smothering silt

These pictures show the devastating effects of deforestation. All over the world, forests are being cut down to satisfy the demand for hardwoods such as teak and mahogany. They are also cut down to make way for farms, or simply to provide local people with firewood and animal feed. The result is the same – bare hillsides, rivers of mud, dams and irrigation systems silted up, and coastal habitats choked with mud.

Replanting

In parts of the Himalayas, mountain slopes have been stripped bare by people desperate for firewood and foliage to feed to their yaks. This Nepalese woman is planting pine seedlings as part of an international project to repair the damaged hillsides and stop soil erosion.

Blooming algae

Rivers carry farm fertilizers from the land to the sea. When they reach the sea, these chemicals also fertilize algae in the water, causing them to grow faster than usual. The pounding surf beats the jelly-like coatings of the algae into a thick, smelly froth, which washes up on our beaches.

TOXIC RUN OFF

EXPERIMENT

You will need: 2 baking trays, a brick, gloves, earth, a trowel, food colouring, water, jug, pieces of turf

1 SET UP THE TRAYS as shown in the picture above. Then fill the sloping tray with an even layer of earth and press it down firmly. Half fill the other tray with water.

2 PLANT SMALL PIECES OF TURF in the soil. Let them grow for a few days to provide vegetation cover.

3 MAKE A HOLE IN THE SOIL at the top of the slope, and put in a few drops of food colouring. This is your "illegal" toxic waste dump. Pour water gently onto the soil.

Colouring is washed through the soil by water

4 SWIRLS OF COLOUR in the lower baking tray reveal the arrival of the water you poured onto the soil – stained by its unwelcome cargo of "pollution".

This shows that: water can wash toxic pollutants out of "safe storage" on the land into rivers and seas.

Blue Peter ACTION!

Only use a small amount of washing-up liquid when you wash the dishes.

Remember that what you throw on the land can eventually make its way to the sea.

Toxic dump

Nobody wants toxic waste on their doorstep. However, rich industrial nations sometimes illegally dump their waste on poorer countries. Here, waste from Italy leaks into the soil in Koko, Nigeria, poisoning the soil where the villagers grow their crops.

FOUL SEA

People have been throwing domestic and farm waste into the sea for thousands of years. Long ago, when the world's population was only a few million, this was not a big problem. The amount of rubbish was small, and the tides and currents soon washed it away. Things are very different now the world population is 6 billion. The amount of rubbish we are dumping is enormous, and a lot of it is dangerous – industrial chemicals, raw sewage, even nuclear waste. Although international laws limit many types of dumping at sea, there is still much to be done in the campaign for cleaner seas.

A supply of **clean water** is essential for all **life**

A thing of the past
The sea turns orange as a ship dumps hundreds of tonnes of jarosite (the waste product of zinc smelting) off the coast of Australia in 1990. The last permit for this kind of dumping ran out in 1997. No new permits have been issued for dumping industrial waste in Australia's waters.

Mineral waste dumped at sea can sink and kill life on the sea floor.

San Francisco bay contains more than **150 foreign** species carried there in ships' **ballast tanks**

Comb jelly

Alien invaders
When ships unload their cargo, they fill their ballast tanks with sea water to add weight and keep them stable. On arrival at the next port, they pump out the ballast water – teeming with "foreign" marine life. The comb jelly shown here was transported from the North Atlantic to the Black Sea where it has thrived and upset the local ecosystem.

Drum full of low-level nuclear waste

Nuclear dumping

This image shows low-level nuclear waste being dumped in the North Sea. This type of waste includes clothing and equipment contaminated with radioactive chemicals that have been used in hospitals and research laboratories. Although dumping of high-level nuclear waste is already banned – it still happens.

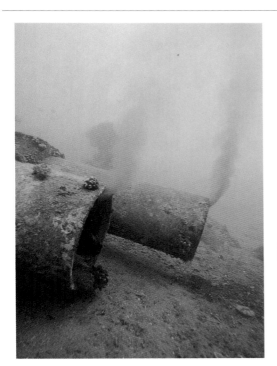

Piped pollution

All over the world, raw sewage is poured into the sea. The sewage feeds bacteria which multiply and deprive other sea creatures of oxygen. It also contains germs that can cause diseases. The problem is worst in developing countries, where there may be no proper sewage treatment plants.

Bacteria in sewage can cause **fatal diseases** such as **cholera**

66 I live in a village called St Agnes on the coast of north Cornwall, England. My life revolves around surfing and the ocean. I go surfing just about every day and it is really important to me that the sea is kept clean. If it is dirty I am at risk of getting ill from the pollution and sewage, along with all the other animals that swim in the water. I try to help by supporting an environmental group called Surfers Against Sewage who campaign to clean the seas. SAS have done a lot for the health of the sea and for surfers since it was first set up. 99

Brennan Cascelles

Surfers against sewage

The water off our coasts is sometimes so full of bacteria from raw sewage that beaches are closed to the public. Many people campaign to clean up the seas, but the loudest protests have come from surfers – the people who suffer most from illnesses caused by sewage. Their actions have persuaded many goverments to clean up their acts.

Plastic dumped in the oceans **kills** an estimated 40,000 **seals** a year

Blue **Peter**
ACTION!

Find out more about organizations that are campaigning for cleaner seas.

Always find out if water is clean before you go swimming in it.

Disaster!

The supertanker

Exxon Valdez struck a reef in Prince William Sound, Alaska, on 24 March 1989. Forty-two million litres (11 million gallons) of crude oil poured into the sea, covering 2,000 km (more than 1,200 miles) of shoreline in a thick, poisonous sludge. People feared that the delicate sea and shoreline habitats would never recover. More than ten years later, the herring shoals and harbour seals have not returned, but the salmon are back, and so are the bald eagles, murres and other seabirds. Slowly, Prince William Sound is beginning to heal.

There have been about 50 oil spills as big as the *Exxon Valdez* since 1970

Boom time

When the tanker *Sea Empress* ran aground in Milford Haven, Wales, in 1996, 72,000 tonnes of oil were spilled. Floating booms like this were used to scoop up about 2,000 tonnes of the oil before it could drift onto the shore. About 36,000 tonnes of oil were dispersed at sea using chemicals sprayed from aircraft.

It takes **years** for coastal **fisheries** to recover from a **major oil spill**

Lightening the load
With the *Exxon Valdez* stuck on Bligh Reef, the disaster team rushed smaller tankers to the scene to pump out 160 million litres (42 million gallons) of oil still in the tanks. This reduced the threat of further spills. It also lightened the tanker so that it could be towed off the reef.

Escort ships now **watch** over **every tanker** as it passes through **Prince William Sound**

Natural protection
A bird feather consists of hundreds of fine strands held together by hooks, or barbules. When a seabird is coated in oil, the hooks are "undone". This ruins the feather's waterproofing and the bird may die. It can take two hours to clean the oil off a single bird.

The big clean-up
After the disaster, it took a massive effort to clean up. An army of 11,000 people, many volunteers, toiled for weeks with high-pressure water jets, rakes, shovels, even paper towels, to mop up oil from the rocks. But nature is the best cleaner. Most of the oil was broken up and washed away by the waves, tides, and currents.

Counting the cost
Scientists can only guess how many birds and mammals died in the *Exxon Valdez* spill. It is always difficult to separate the direct effects of an oil spill from natural fluctuations caused by diseases and other factors.

OIL AND FEATHERS
EXPERIMENT

You will need: rubber gloves, a plate, water, 2 bunches of bird feathers, cooking oil, cotton wool, washing-up liquid.

1 **POUR A LITTLE** water onto a plate. Pour some oil onto the surface. Dip both bunches of feathers into the oily water to imitate what happens when a seabird lands on an oil slick in the sea.

Wear gloves when handling feathers.

2 **CLEAN ONE BUNCH** of feathers using just water and cotton wool. Clean the other bunch using water mixed with washing-up liquid.

Feathers cleaned with water

Feathers cleaned with washing-up liquid

3 **EXAMINE THE FEATHERS.** Those cleaned with water alone are still matted and heavy. The others are cleaner and lighter.

This shows that: washing an oiled bird with water and washing-up liquid gives it the best chance. Even so, cleaned birds can still die of cold.

Killer whales
About 20 died, probably from eating fish contaminated with oil.

Sea otters
Up to 5,000 died. Many also left because of local food shortages.

Harbour seals
Up to 300 died. The figures could be higher as seals sink when dead.

Seabirds
Up to half a million died. Some species are still not recovering.

MARINE IMPACT SPECIALIST
DR JULIAN GALLOWAY

JULIAN GALLOWAY TRAVELS ALL OVER THE WORLD FOR HIS JOB. HIS WORK INVOLVES LOOKING AT HOW DEVELOPMENTS, SUCH AS PORTS AND HARBOURS, or structures including oil and gas platforms, will affect the local environment. His years of training as an oceanographer help him to carry out these studies.

Oil delivery
A tanker unloads its cargo of oil at a jetty. Any oil spill can harm sea life.

A day in the life of a
MARINE IMPACT SPECIALIST

As the coasts come under increasing pressure from developers, it is often scientists who can help to limit any damage to the environment.

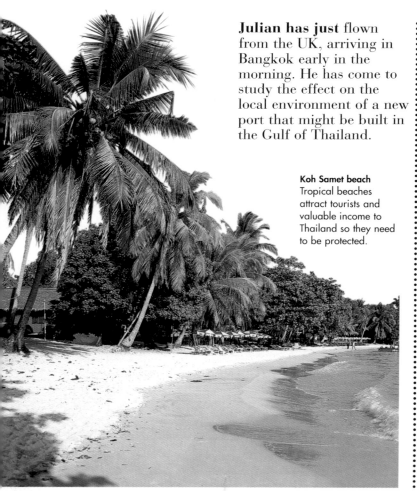

Koh Samet beach
Tropical beaches attract tourists and valuable income to Thailand so they need to be protected.

Julian has just flown from the UK, arriving in Bangkok early in the morning. He has come to study the effect on the local environment of a new port that might be built in the Gulf of Thailand.

5:30am First thing I do on arrival is to collect several pieces of marine survey equipment at the airport. Then I drive to Rayong on the Gulf of Thailand to meet up with colleagues. We load the current meter, water quality-testing instruments, and seabed scanners onto a local boat. Because it is quite a drop down from the jetty to the boat, we tie ropes around the boxes and two of us lower the equipment.

7:30am Before leaving, we test the equipment on the boat. We then sail 4 km (2.5 miles) down the coast to a jetty where ships unload cargoes of oil and fish. This is where two more jetties and a breakwater – to create a new port – might be built.

9:00am We begin collecting water samples from the sea surface using special bottles. These will be sent back to the laboratory in the UK. Scientists will measure

Map of Thailand
Rayong is an important area for tourism as well as nature conservation.

the amount of oil, toxic metals, and other chemicals that indicate pollution levels. I use a special piece of equipment (called a multi-parameter probe) to measure the temperature and saltiness of the sea. It also measures levels of oxygen and sediment (loose material). The information will help me understand the health of local coral reefs and fish. To take these readings, I attach a probe to a

Current meter
This measures the speed and direction of water movement.

> **My work draws together many different skills – biology, geology, engineering, and oceanography.**

small computer using a waterproof cable. Then I tie a weight to the probe, and use a rope to lower it into the water. I take measurements at the sea surface, and at every metre (yard) as I lower the probe. Meanwhile, my colleagues check water movement with a current meter.

10:30am Next we measure the shape of the seabed with an echo sounder and side-scan sonar. This will help us study how sediments move near the coral reef. The echo sounder looks straight down to the seabed, but the side-scan sonar looks out at an angle. The sonar is called a "fish" because it has fins to help it travel smoothly through the water. Because the "fish" is very heavy, we lower it into the water with a winch and cable.

11:30am We move on to a well-known coral reef called Koh Samet. Tourists go there to watch the reef fish and admire the shapes and

Dredger at work
Dredging the water stirs up sediment in the water, which can kill coral and force fish to move elsewhere.

colours of the corals. Once there, we use an underwater video camera to film the fish and corals. Later we will use the video tape to make a list of all the fish and corals we have seen. This helps us understand the range of marine life in the area.

1:00pm We stop work for lunch on the boat. I study the information on water quality, seabed shape, fish, and coral reef. This will help me plan the new port with least impact on the marine ecosystem. For example, we may need to take into account seasonal currents when dredging. I'm worried that dredgers could disturb sand on the seabed. The reef could be killed, with important fish moving away from the area. I decide to travel to a nearby port to study how that was built.

4:00pm Map Ta Phut Port is down the coast from Rayong. The planned new port will be similar to this one. After studying the port area, I meet the people in charge and talk about how they intend to build the new one. I tell them I am worried about the coral reef, and that the local environment protection department should be

Desolate beach
Construction work scars a beach, but with good planning it can be restored.

told. The managers explain that the new port is important as it will provide vital jobs for local people. They also tell me that the fish industry is a big employer because nam pla – a fish paste used in Thai cooking – is made in Rayong.

5:00pm We travel back to our hotel very tired. I use my computer to predict what the sediment disturbance might be on the reef and fish. I was right to be worried – a lot of sand could fall on the reef and damage the coral. This is because sand stops light, which coral needs to survive, from getting through. I test a new way of building the port. This time my computer shows the sediment moving harmlessly away from the reef. With care, and new building methods, the port could be built with no damage to the reef and fish. Pleased that the local people may have new jobs at a new port, make fish paste, and enjoy the coral reef, I sit down to write up my report.

Life in the coral
The reefs in the shallow waters off Thailand are among the richest in the world.

Underwater camera
Counting fish and coral species is easier when they are recorded on video.

Side-scan sonar
This instrument uses sound waves to map the shape of the seabed.

A major sea level rise could affect 72 million people in China alone

RISING SEA LEVELS

Global warming

Carbon dioxide, water vapour, and methane are the main "greenhouse" gases. Like the panes of a greenhouse, they let the Sun's energy (and heat) in, and then trap some of it. Without them, we would freeze. But vehicle exhausts, factory emissions, and forest burning have added too much extra. The greenhouse is now too efficient, and the Earth is overheating.

One of the biggest questions that needs to be answered by environmental scientists is "How much will sea levels rise as a result of global warming?" They know that rises in global temperatures will do two things. It will make the water in the oceans expand, so that sea levels will rise a bit. It could also melt some or all of the polar ice caps. This would add huge amounts of water to the oceans, making them rise very much more. The Earth has been warming slowly for 7,000 years. The problem is that human activities over the past 150 years have been making its temperature rise faster and faster.

MELTING ICE CAPS

You will need: 2 identical glass bowls, tray, 2 unopened food cans, jug, water, ice cubes, marker tape.

1 PLACE THE BOWLS on a tray with a can inside each one. Part fill the first bowl with water, add plenty of ice, and mark the water level with tape. Mark the same level on the second bowl and fill up to the mark with water.

2 PILE ICE CUBES on top of the can in the second bowl, but do not put any ice in the water. You have created one "island" surrounded by "sea ice" and one covered by an "ice cap".

3 LEAVE THE ICE to melt. Notice that the water level in the first bowl is the same, but the "sea level" in the second bowl has risen.

This shows that: when sea ice melts, the water does not take up any extra volume. But when land ice melts, water levels rise.

Cracks in the ice

Over the past few years, huge chunks have broken away from the floating ice shelves around Antarctica. The cause is a rise in sea temperature – and it is a serious warning to us all. When floating ice melts, sea levels do not change. But if the ice caps that cover land start to melt, the world is in trouble because sea levels will rise.

Parts of **London** could flood if **sea levels** rise **3 m (10 ft)**

GEORGIA

ATLANTIC OCEAN

FLORIDA

GULF OF MEXICO

•Cape Canaveral

The Everglades •West Palm Beach

•Miami

☐ Florida coastline

☐ Florida after flooding

Florida Keys

Florida's rising sea levels

Low-lying coastal areas around the world are at risk from sea level rise. In Florida (left) a rise of 7.5 m (25 ft) would swamp vast areas of the state, including Miami and West Palm Beach. Elsewhere in the world, cities such as Amsterdam, Bombay, and Sydney would vanish beneath the water.

The flood threat

Millions of Bangladeshis in the lowlands of the Ganges delta suffer from flooding caused by monsoon rains and hurricanes. If sea levels rise, millions of hectares of their low-lying coastal farmland could disappear forever under a shallow, salty sea.

Half the **world's population** lives in **low-lying coastal** areas

Sea defences

Low-lying, developed countries, such as the Netherlands, already spend huge amounts of money building sea defences. These walls prevent sea water from spilling onto the land. If sea levels rise they will need to be far higher and cover longer stretches of coast.

Sea wall under construction

Action Plan

IF YOU CARE ABOUT THE OCEANS and want to help save their natural environment, there are many organizations that will help you to get involved. This list includes those you can contact in the UK, as well as international organizations you can visit on the internet.

BBC Nature
A website with news, tv programme follow-ups, competitions, events, and factfiles all relating to the natural world.

www.bbc.co.uk/nature

BBC Science
Information about the oceans and marine science, from climate-change threats and coral reefs to pollution.

www.bbc.co.uk/science

BirdLife International
A leading bird conservation organization with branches worldwide. Promotes campaigns for improving the protection of threatened species and habitats.

Wellbrook Court
Girton Road
Cambridge CB3 0NA

British Antarctic Survey
An organization responsible for the UK's scientific research in Antarctica and the Southern Ocean. The website gives full details of current research programmes.

www.antarctica.ac.uk

High Cross
Madingley Road
Cambridge CB3 0ET

British Marine Life Study Society
Readable and informative articles on marine life and the ocean environment around the British Isles.

http//ourworld.compuserve.com/
homepages/BMLSS

Glaucus House
14 Corbyn Crescent
Shoreham-by-Sea
Sussex BN43 6PQ

California Coastal Conservancy
An organization that helps preserve, protect, and restore the resources of the California Coast.

www.coastalconservancy.ca.gov

1330 Broadway
11th Floor
Oakland
CA 94612 USA

The Coral Reef Alliance
Promotes coral reef conservation around the world by supporting protection efforts and raising public awareness.

www.coral.org

2014 Shattuck Avenue
Berkeley
CA 94704 USA

Countryside Council for Wales
Service responsible for the variety of wild plants and animals, the natural landscape and biodiversity in Wales.

www.ccw.gov.uk

English Nature
The statutory service responsible for the variety of wild plants and animals, the natural landscape and biodiversity in England.

www.english-nature.org.uk

Environmental Investigation Agency
An international organization committed to investigating environmental crime and changing the law to protect endangered species and habitats.

www.eia-international.org

69 Old Street
London EC1V 9HX

Friends of the Earth
International network of environmental groups that commissions research and campaigns for changes in the law.

www.foe.co.uk

26-28 Underwood Street
London, N1 7JQ

Great American Fish Count
A US-based programme that makes use of volunteer divers to study fish populations and marine habitats.

www.fishcount.org

Greenpeace
One of the world's leading environmental organizations, involved in direct action to safeguard the planet's future.

www.greenpeace.org

International Union for the Conservation of Nature and Natural Resources (IUCN)
The world's largest conservation-related organization that brings together 76 states and many other groups in a unique worldwide partnership

www.iucn.org

The Marine Conservation Society
UK-based charity for the marine environment and its wildlife. Pages of fascinating facts and photos, the latest news on marine issues and ways to get involved. Website gives a list of Britain's cleanest beaches.

www.mcsuk.org

MarLIN (The Marine Life Information Network for Britain and Ireland)
A comprehensive source of information about marine habitats, communities and species around Britain and Ireland.

www.marlin.ac.uk

Project Seahorse
Programme of seahorse management, involving community action, practical conservation, and scientific study of seahorses and their habitats.

www.projectseahorse.org

Seaweb
Web-based project where you can find all the latest news stories about the ocean environment.

www.seaweb.org

Scottish Natural Heritage
Service responsible for the variety of wild plants and animals, the natural landscape and biodiversity in Scotland.

www.snh.org.uk

Surfers Against Sewage
Active grass-roots campaign to stop marine sewage and toxic waste discharge into waters around Britain.

www.sas.org.uk

2 Rural Workshops
Wheal Kitty
St Agnes
Cornwall TR5 0RD

Tourism Concern
Promotes awareness of the impact of tourism on the environment.

www.tourismconcern.org.uk

Stapleton House
277-281 Holloway Road
London N7 8HN

United Nations Environment Programme (UNEP)
The UN agency founded in 1972 to safeguard and enhance the environment for present and future generations.

www.unep.org

World Conservation Monitoring Centre
Collects and publishes information about the world's endangered species, as well as environmental issues.

www.wcmc.org.uk

219 Huntingdon Road
Cambridge CB3 0DL

Worldwide Fund for Nature (WWF)
The world's largest conservation organization. Visit the website to find out about what the WWF does, and to check out the Living Planet Report.

www.panda.org

Panda House
Weyside Park
Godalming
Surrey GU7 2XR

THE GREEN BLUE PETER BADGE

As you read this book, planet Earth – along with all the oceans and seas – is under threat. But it is not too late to save the Earth and you, the children of today, will be the people who shape the future.

When you put the ideas in the Action Globes into practice you will be playing an important part in changing the world for the better and you could also earn yourself a Green *Blue Peter* Badge.

Since we launched the Green *Blue Peter* Badge on the programme in 1988, we have been flooded with letters, ideas, drawings, and poems from children across Britain who care about the environment. We know that this book will only be as helpful in saving the planet as the people who read it, so now it's up to you.

LET US KNOW
what you think and what you are up to by writing to *Blue Peter* at:

BLUE **PETER**
BBC Television Centre
Wood Lane
London W12 7RJ

www.bbc.co.uk/bluepeter

You can also use the internet to contact the programme, via our e-mail address:

bluepeter@bbc.co.uk

Index

Credits

Dorling Kindersley would like to thank:
Sheila Hanly for locating many of the Day in the Life experts; Amanda Carroll, Sheila Collins, Sharon Grant, Claire Legemah, Keith Newell, Peter Radcliffe, and Laura Roberts for design help; Lynn Bresler, index.

Andy Crawford for photography of the experiments, and models Harriet Couchman and Dejaune Davis.

Special thanks to Day in the Life experts and their organizations who provided many free photographs – Carl Meyer (Marine Biologist); Keith Saunders (Fisheries Protection Officer); Amanda Vincent (Seahorse Specialist); Keiran Copeland (Marine Mammal Medic); Julian Galloway (Marine Impact Specialist). Thanks to the AOC, REEF, and US NOAA Marine Sanctuary Program.

Additional photography: Geoff Brightling, Jane Burton, Steve Gorton, Frank Greenaway, Dave King, Ray Moller, Andreas von Einsiedel, Alex Wilson. Models: Martin Camm, Peter Griffiths, Peter Minister.

Picture Credits
The publishers would like to thank the following for their kind permission to reproduce the photographs:
a = above; c = centre; b = bottom; l = left; r = right;
t = top; f = far; n = near.

Heather Angel: 15bc. **Ardea London Ltd:** 43c; Chris Knights 43bl; Hans D. Dossenbach 37bl; John Mason 21br; K.W. Fink 53bl. **Tomas Bertelsen:** 34tl. **Bruce Coleman Ltd:** 12, 32b; Derek Croucher 36b; Fred Bruemmer 32br; Gerald S. Cubitt 42l; John Cancalosi 33c, 33br, 37cb; Mark N. Boulton 36-37t; Neil McAllister 31cl; Nicholas Devore 46tr; Thomas Buchholz 54bl. **Colorific!:** Philippe Hays 57br. © Crown Copyright: Historic Royal Palaces 1999: 15t. **DK Picture Library:** Apple Macintosh 18cr. **Brad Doane:** 22b. **Edgetech:** 55br. **Environmental Images:** 49bl; Alex Olah 49tl; Chris Martin 26tr; Daniel Beltra 43tl; David Hoffman 47cbl; Herbert Girardet 56cr; Peter Rowlands 23br; Pierre Gleizes 51tr; Richard Smith 38tl; Roger Grace 31tr; Steve Morgan 20cl, 20bc, 57tl. **Greenpeace Inc:** Hewetson 50-51; Matoff 11bl. **Robert Harding Picture Library:** 33tr; Guy Thouvenin 33bl. **Hutchison Library:** 47tc. **Hyder Consulting:** 54tl, 54br, 54-55, 55tr, 55cl. **Image Bank:** Paul McCormick 37br. **Institute of Marine Biology, Hawaii:** 18tl, 18-19, 19tr, 19cl. **Japanese Meteorological Agency/Meteorological Office:** 14tl, 14tcl, 14tcr. **Kos Pictures Source:** Gilles Martin-Raget 38-39b. **FLPA - Images of Nature:** D. P. Wilson 47cl; Ron Austing 14cr. **Jessica Meeuwig, Research Scientist, Project Seahorse:** 34bl. **Don Merton:** 33cl. **Natural History Museum, London:** 7br. **N.H.P.A.:** John Shaw 42cbr; Norbert Wu 16clb, 22-23; Roger Tidman 33tt. **Oxford Scientific Films:** Doug Allan 48tl; John Brown 13tl; Laurence Gould 8t; Mark Webster 30-31, 58-59; Michael Pitts 50br. **Panos Pictures:** R.Berriedale-Johnson 38bl. **Planet Earth Pictures:** 12-13; C. Maddock 27cr; Chris Prior 32-33tl; Darroch Donald 53cb; Doug Perrine 43cr; Gary Bell 2-3;

Ivor Edmonds 16cr; Jeannie Mackinnon 48bl; Kurt Amsler 28-29; Norbert Wu 50cb; Patrick de Wilde 13br; Richard Chesher 15cr; Warren Williams 51tl. **Popperfoto:** Rafiqur Rahman 56-57b. **Rex Features:** 23tr. **Michael Ricketts:** 34br. **Keith Saunders, Fisheries Western Australia:** 24tl, 24cl, 24bl, 24-25, 25tr, 25cr. **Science Photo Library:** Astrid & Hanns-Frieder Michler 16tl; Douglas Faulkner 6-7, 28-29; Gene Feldman 16tr; Martin Bond 13cr; Vanessa Vick 53cl. **SOS Seal Rescue Hospital, Hunstanton:** 40tl, 40cb, 40br, 41tr, 41cla, 41crb, 41bl. **Still Pictures:** Al Grillo 53tl; Dylan Garcia 45bl; Fred Dott 26-27; Hanson Carroll 17cl; Hartmut Schwarzbach 56tc; Jean-Luc Zeigler 47bl; Kelvin Aitken 39c; Marilyn Kazmers 31cr; Mark Edwards 48cl; Nigel Dickinson 15cr; Norbert Wu 53bc, 53bc; Ray Pfortner 37cl; Roland Seitre 39tr; Ron Giling 22l; Somboon-Unep 27cl; Thomas Raupach 49cl; Yves Lefevre 19b. **Tony Stone Images:** Art Wolfe 21cl; Bob Torrez 51br; David Woodfall 52l; Norbert Wu 6tl, 10-11; Warren Bolster 7tr, 44-45. **Sygma:** 14b. **Amanda Vincent, Project Seahorse:** 34crb, 34-35, 35cl, 35cr. **Chris Woods:** National Institute of Water and Atmosphere Research, Wellington, New Zealand 35b.

Jacket Credits

Environmental Images: Richard Smith front bl; Roger Grace front bc. **Robert Harding Picture Library:** Back bc. **N.H.P.A.:** A.N.T front c. **Oxford Scientific Films:** John Brown back cla. **Science Photo Library:** Douglas Faulkner inside back; Gene Feldman/NASA GSFC back cla. **Still Pictures:** Dylan Garcia back cra; Marilyn Kazmers back bl. **Tony Stone Images:** Art Wolfe inside front ; Steve Barnett front br.